Table of contents

Part 1: The Early Years

A Star is Born

Cherilyn Sarkisian, the woman the world would come to know simply as Cher, entered the world on May 20, 1946, in El Centro, California. Her birthplace, a small desert town near the Mexican border, offered little hint of the glamorous future that awaited her. Her early life was marked by instability, a stark contrast to the glitz and glamour she would later embody.

Cher's parentage was a mix of cultures and complexities. Her father, John Sarkisian, was an Armenian-American truck driver with a penchant for gambling and struggles with addiction. Her mother, Georgia Holt (born Jackie Jean Crouch), was a striking beauty with dreams of stardom, working as a model and aspiring actress. Holt's ancestry, a

CHER

BIOGRAPHY

CLIFF SOWLE

Disclaimer:

This is a work of nonfiction. All efforts have been made to provide accurate information, but some events or conversations may be reconstructed based on available sources and the author's research. Any errors or omissions are unintentional.

blend of Irish, English, German, and Cherokee, contributed to Cher's unique and captivating looks.

Cher's parents' relationship was tumultuous, marked by frequent separations and reconciliations. When Cher was just ten months old, they divorced, setting the stage for a childhood punctuated by upheaval and uncertainty. Financial hardship forced Georgia to temporarily place Cher in an orphanage while she sought work. This early experience, though brief, likely left a lasting impression on the young Cher, highlighting the precarious nature of her circumstances.

Georgia, determined to provide for her daughter, embarked on a series of marriages, each offering a fleeting sense of stability. She had another daughter, Georganne, with one of her husbands, adding a half-sister to Cher's life. The family moved frequently, from California to Oklahoma to Texas, as Georgia pursued acting opportunities and sought to build a better life.

This nomadic lifestyle exposed Cher to a diverse range of people and places, shaping her worldview and fostering a sense of adaptability. Despite the challenges, Georgia instilled in her daughters a love of the arts and a belief in the power of self-expression. She encouraged Cher's early interest in performing, enrolling her in acting classes and securing her small roles as an extra in television shows like *The Adventures of Ozzie and Harriet*.

Even as a young girl, Cher possessed a captivating presence and a natural flair for the dramatic. She was drawn to the spotlight, often entertaining her classmates with impromptu performances. Her distinctive voice, deep and resonant even then, set her apart. Though she struggled with undiagnosed dyslexia, which made traditional schooling a challenge, she found solace and confidence in the performing arts.

At the age of 16, Cher, eager to escape the constraints of her unstable home life and pursue her dreams, dropped out of high school and moved to Los Angeles. It was a bold move, driven by a fierce ambition and an unwavering belief in her own potential. She took acting classes, worked odd jobs to support herself, and immersed herself in the vibrant cultural scene of 1960s Hollywood.

It was during this time, in 1962, that Cher's life took a dramatic turn. She met Salvatore "Sonny" Bono, a charismatic aspiring musician and record producer, at a coffee shop on Sunset Boulevard. This chance encounter would forever alter the course of her life, launching her on a trajectory to stardom and shaping the first chapter of her extraordinary career.

Cher's early life was a complex mix woven with threads of instability, resilience, and an innate passion for performing. Her unconventional upbringing, marked by financial struggles, frequent moves, and her parents' turbulent relationship, instilled in her a sense of independence and a determination to forge her own path. These early experiences, though often challenging, laid the foundation for the strong, self-reliant woman and iconic performer she would become. Her childhood, far from the fairytale often associated with stardom, serves as a testament to her innate talent, her unwavering drive, and her ability to overcome adversity to achieve her dreams.

Meeting Sonny

Los Angeles in the early 1960s was a magnet for young dreamers, and Cher, at the age of 16, was no exception. She'd arrived with a head full of ambition and a heart set on making it big, but the path to stardom was far from clear. Working odd jobs and attending acting classes, she was just another face in the crowd, hoping for a lucky break. That break came in the form of a chance meeting with Salvatore "Sonny" Bono, a man who would become her musical partner, husband, and the catalyst for her rise to fame.

Their first encounter was far from glamorous. It was 1962, and Cher, still a teenager, was frequenting a coffee shop on Sunset Boulevard, a popular hangout for musicians and industry hopefuls. Sonny, eleven years her senior and already working as a promoter and songwriter for Phil Spector's record label, was a regular at the café. He spotted Cher, drawn in by her striking looks and unconventional style, and struck up a conversation.

Despite their age difference and contrasting personalities, they formed an instant connection. Sonny, with his outgoing nature and show business savvy, was the opposite of the shy and insecure Cher. He recognized her raw talent and star potential, while she was drawn to his confidence and ambition. He offered her a place to stay, and soon, their platonic friendship blossomed into a romantic relationship.

United by their love of music and their desire for success, Cher and Sonny began collaborating creatively. Sonny, with his songwriting skills and industry connections, saw in Cher the perfect vehicle for his musical ambitions. He encouraged her to sing, recognizing the power and uniqueness of her voice. Initially, she sang backup on several recordings produced by Sonny, including tracks for artists like the Ronettes and the Righteous Brothers.

Their big break came when Sonny secured Cher a solo recording contract with Imperial Records. Her first single,

"Ringo, I Love You," released in 1964 under the pseudonym Bonnie Jo Mason, failed to make a significant impact. However, it marked the beginning of her recording career and solidified her partnership with Sonny, who was now acting as her producer and manager.

Recognizing the magic of their combined talents, they decided to perform as a duo. Sonny & Cher, as they became known, embodied the spirit of the 1960s youth culture. Their contrasting looks – Sonny's clean-cut appearance juxtaposed with Cher's bohemian style – and their playful banter on stage created a captivating dynamic. Their music, a blend of folk, pop, and rock, resonated with a generation yearning for something new and different.

Their breakthrough came in 1965 with the release of "I Got You Babe." The song, written by Sonny, became an instant sensation, topping the charts in the United States and the United Kingdom. It captured the essence of young love and the optimistic spirit of the era, making Sonny & Cher household names.

The success of "I Got You Babe" launched them into the stratosphere of pop stardom. They followed it up with a string of hits, including "Baby Don't Go" and "The Beat Goes On," solidifying their status as musical icons. They appeared on television shows, toured extensively, and even starred in their own movie, *Good Times*, in 1967.

Sonny & Cher became synonymous with the 1960s, their music and fashion choices influencing youth culture on both sides of the Atlantic. They represented a new era of pop music, one that embraced social change and challenged traditional norms. Their partnership, both personal and professional, had transformed them from aspiring artists into global superstars.

The meeting between Cher and Sonny Bono was a pivotal moment, not just in their individual lives, but in the history of pop music. Their connection sparked a creative partnership that would produce some of the most iconic songs of the 1960s. Sonny's belief in Cher's talent, combined with their shared ambition and their ability to connect with audiences, laid the foundation for their extraordinary success. Their story is a testament to the power of collaboration, the allure of stardom, and the enduring magic of pop music.

"I Got You Babe" and the Sonny & Cher Phenomenon

The year 1965 marked a turning point in the trajectory of Sonny & Cher. Their unique blend of folk-rock, infused with Sonny's songwriting talent and Cher's distinctive vocals, found its perfect expression in the song "I Got You Babe." This simple yet powerful love song captured the zeitgeist of the era, propelling them to the forefront of the music scene and solidifying their place in pop culture history.

"I Got You Babe" was more than just a catchy tune; it was a cultural phenomenon. Released in the summer of 1965, it quickly climbed the charts, reaching the number one spot in both the United States and the United Kingdom. Its infectious melody, combined with the heartfelt lyrics and the undeniable chemistry between Sonny & Cher, resonated with audiences worldwide.

The song's success was fueled by its widespread exposure on radio and television. Sonny & Cher's appearances on popular music programs like *American Bandstand* and *The Ed Sullivan Show* introduced them to a wider audience, further amplifying the song's popularity. The music video for "I Got You Babe," featuring the duo strolling through a picturesque park, became an early example of the power of visual media in promoting music.

The appeal of "I Got You Babe" extended beyond its musical merits. The song's lyrics, expressing unwavering love and devotion in the face of societal disapproval, struck a chord with young people navigating the changing social landscape of the 1960s. It became an anthem for a generation embracing new ideas about love, relationships, and personal freedom.

Sonny & Cher's image also played a significant role in their success. Their contrasting styles – Sonny's neat and conventional appearance juxtaposed with Cher's flowing hair, bell bottoms, and Native American-inspired attire – created a visual dynamic that was both captivating and unconventional. They challenged traditional gender roles and fashion norms, becoming style icons for a generation eager to break free from the constraints of the past.

"I Got You Babe" was not a one-hit wonder. Sonny & Cher followed it up with a series of successful singles, including "Baby Don't Go," "The Beat Goes On," and "Little Man." These songs further cemented their status as pop music royalty and showcased their versatility as artists.

Their music, with its catchy melodies and relatable themes, became the soundtrack of the 1960s youth movement. Their influence extended beyond music, shaping fashion trends, television programming, and even social attitudes. They were pioneers in creating a multimedia presence, starring in their own television variety show, *The Sonny & Cher Comedy Hour*, which further amplified their popularity and solidified their status as cultural icons.

The impact of "I Got You Babe" and the Sonny & Cher phenomenon can still be felt today. The song remains a beloved classic, frequently featured in movies, television shows, and commercials. Their music continues to be enjoyed by new generations, and their influence on fashion and popular culture is undeniable.

Sonny & Cher's rise to fame was a testament to their ability to connect with audiences on a personal level. They captured the spirit of a generation with their music, their style, and their message of love and acceptance. Their legacy serves as a reminder of the power of pop music to reflect and shape cultural trends, and their story remains an inspiring example of how talent, ambition, and a bit of luck can lead to extraordinary success.

Beyond the Music

While their musical success was undeniable, Sonny & Cher were not content to be confined to the recording studio. They possessed a natural charisma and comedic timing that translated seamlessly to television, leading them to conquer a new medium and further solidify their status as entertainment icons.

Even before "I Got You Babe" catapulted them to stardom, Sonny & Cher were making inroads into the world of television. They appeared on popular variety shows like *American Bandstand* and *The Ed Sullivan Show*, showcasing their musical talents and engaging in playful banter with the hosts.[1] These early appearances provided a glimpse of their comedic potential and their ability to connect with audiences beyond their music.

Their growing popularity led to guest spots on sitcoms and talk shows, including *The Love Boat* and *The Mike Douglas Show*.[2] These appearances allowed them to showcase their personalities and expand their fan base. Sonny, with his quick wit and self-deprecating humor, often played the foil to Cher's dry humor and sarcastic remarks. Their on-screen chemistry was undeniable, and audiences were drawn to their playful dynamic.

In 1971, Sonny & Cher took a major leap forward with their own television variety show, *The Sonny & Cher Comedy Hour*.[3] This weekly program featured a mix of musical performances, comedic sketches, and celebrity guest appearances.[4] It quickly became a ratings hit, capturing the attention of millions of viewers each week.[5]

The show's success was due in large part to the undeniable chemistry between Sonny & Cher. Their comedic sketches, often poking fun at their relationship and their contrasting personalities, were a highlight of the show. Cher's glamorous costumes, designed by Bob Mackie, became a talking point, further enhancing her image as a fashion icon.[6]

The show also featured a talented supporting cast, including Teri Garr, Freeman King, and Ted Zeigler.[7] Musical guests ranged from contemporary pop stars to legendary figures like Tony Bennett and Tina Turner.[8] The variety format allowed Sonny & Cher to showcase their versatility, moving effortlessly between musical performances, comedic sketches, and interactions with guests.[9]

The Sonny & Cher Comedy Hour became a cultural touchstone, capturing the spirit of the early 1970s. It was a time of social change and experimentation, and the show reflected this with its mix of humor, music, and social commentary. Sonny & Cher's willingness to address topical issues, albeit in a lighthearted manner, resonated with audiences and contributed to the show's popularity.

The show's influence extended beyond entertainment. It helped to popularize the variety show format, paving the way for similar programs like *Donny & Marie* and *The Captain & Tennille*. It also showcased the talents of its supporting cast, launching the careers of several actors and comedians.

Despite its success, *The Sonny & Cher Comedy Hour* came to an end in 1974, coinciding with the couple's divorce.[10]However, their television careers continued. Cher went on to host her own variety show, *Cher*, while Sonny briefly had his own show, *The Sonny Comedy Revue*. They even reunited for a short-lived revival of *The Sonny & Cher Show* in the mid-1970s.[11]

Sonny & Cher's foray into television was a natural extension of their musical talents and their captivating personalities. *The Sonny & Cher Comedy Hour* became a defining program of the early 1970s, showcasing their comedic timing, musical versatility, and undeniable chemistry. Their success on the small screen further solidified their status as entertainment icons, demonstrating their ability to adapt and thrive in a constantly evolving media landscape.

Part 2: Breaking Free

Solo Ambitions

While Sonny & Cher enjoyed immense success as a duo, Cher harbored a burning desire to establish herself as an independent artist. She possessed a unique voice and a stage presence that begged to be explored beyond the confines of their partnership. However, breaking free from the established Sonny & Cher brand and forging her own path proved to be a challenging and often tumultuous journey.

Cher's solo ambitions were evident even during the peak of Sonny & Cher's success. She released her first solo album, *All I Really Want to Do*, in 1965, the same year "I Got You Babe" topped the charts.[1] The album, primarily featuring cover songs, showcased her vocal versatility and hinted at her potential as a solo artist.[2]

While her early solo efforts achieved moderate success, they were often overshadowed by the overwhelming popularity of Sonny & Cher. Sonny, who also acted as her producer and manager, exerted significant control over her musical direction, often choosing songs that fit the established Sonny & Cher sound. This limited Cher's ability to explore her own artistic identity and express her individuality.

Cher's desire for creative control led to tensions within her personal and professional relationship with Sonny. He was accustomed to being the driving force behind their success, and he struggled to relinquish control and allow Cher to fully blossom as a solo artist. Their conflicting visions for her career contributed to the growing strain on their marriage.

Furthermore, the music industry in the 1960s and 70s was not particularly welcoming to female artists seeking autonomy. Women were often expected to conform to established norms and rely on male producers and songwriters to guide their careers. Cher's determination to break free from these expectations and chart her own course was met with resistance and skepticism.

Despite these challenges, Cher persisted in her pursuit of solo success.[3] She released a string of albums throughout the late 1960s and early 1970s, experimenting with different musical styles and pushing the boundaries of her vocal range. Albums like *With Love, Cher* and *Cher* showcased her growth as an artist and her willingness to take risks.

As Cher's solo career progressed, she began to assert more control over her artistic direction. She collaborated with different producers and songwriters, exploring a wider range of musical genres, from pop and folk to disco and rock. This experimentation allowed her to discover her own unique sound and establish a distinct identity separate from Sonny & Cher.

Her determination to break free from the constraints of her partnership with Sonny ultimately led to the dissolution of their marriage in 1974. This painful separation marked a turning point in Cher's life and career. It allowed her to fully embrace her independence and pursue her artistic vision without limitations.

Cher's journey as a solo artist was marked by both ambition and adversity. Her desire to establish her own identity and break free from the shadow of Sonny & Cher was met with challenges and setbacks. However, her persistence, her willingness to experiment, and her unwavering belief in her own talent ultimately led her to achieve solo success and solidify her status as a musical icon.

Her story serves as an inspiration to artists seeking to define their own path and overcome the limitations imposed by others.

Finding Her Voice

Cher's solo career was a journey of self-discovery, a constant evolution of musical styles and artistic expression. She refused to be pigeonholed, embracing diverse genres and pushing the boundaries of her vocal abilities.[1] From her folk-rock roots to her foray into disco, Cher's early solo albums reveal a fearless artist determined to find her own unique voice.

Cher's initial solo work reflected the prevailing sounds of the 1960s, with a strong emphasis on folk-rock and pop. Her first solo album, *All I Really Want to Do* (1965), featured covers of popular folk songs, showcasing her interpretive skills and her ability to connect with the youth culture of the time.

Her subsequent albums, such as *The Sonny Side of Chér* (1966) and *With Love, Chér* (1967), continued in this vein, blending folk-inspired melodies with pop sensibilities.[2] These albums featured songs written by Sonny Bono, but they also allowed Cher to explore her own vocal range and express her individuality.

As the 1960s progressed, Cher's music began to incorporate more pop elements. Albums like *Backstage* (1968) and *3614 Jackson Highway* (1969) featured a mix of original songs and covers, showcasing her versatility and her growing confidence as a solo artist.[3]

While these albums achieved moderate success, they struggled to break free from the shadow of Sonny & Cher. Cher's desire to explore different musical styles and assert her own artistic vision led to creative tensions with Sonny, who continued to exert control over her career.

The 1970s brought a wave of change to the music industry, and Cher was quick to embrace the new sounds of disco. Her album *Gypsys, Tramps & Thieves* (1971) marked a significant departure from her earlier work, featuring a more polished production and a dance-oriented sound.[4]

The album's title track became a massive hit, topping the charts and establishing Cher as a force to be reckoned with in the disco era. Her powerful vocals and theatrical stage presence were perfectly suited to the high-energy rhythms and glamorous aesthetics of disco.[5]

She continued to explore this genre with albums like *Half-Breed* (1973) and *Dark Lady* (1974), both of which spawned chart-topping singles and solidified her status as a disco queen. These albums showcased her vocal prowess and her ability to connect with a wider audience.

Cher's musical journey was not confined to any single genre. She continued to experiment throughout the 1970s and beyond, incorporating elements of rock, pop, and even country into her music. Her willingness to take risks and defy expectations kept her sound fresh and relevant.

Her later albums, such as *Take Me Home* (1979) and *Prisoner* (1979), showcased her continued evolution as an artist.[6]She embraced a more rock-oriented sound, collaborating with leading producers and songwriters to create music that reflected her changing tastes and her growing confidence.

Cher's early solo career was an evidence to her versatility and her unwavering determination to find her own voice. She fearlessly explored different musical styles, from folk-rock to disco, refusing to be confined by genre limitations or industry expectations. Her constant evolution as an artist laid the foundation for her enduring success and solidified her status as a true musical chameleon.

Love and Loss

Cher's life has been a whirlwind of passionate romances and heartbreaking losses, a testament to her capacity for love and her resilience in the face of adversity. Her relationships, often played out in the public eye, have shaped her personal and artistic journey, adding another layer of complexity to the "Goddess of Pop."

Cher's most significant and complex relationship was undoubtedly with Sonny Bono. Their connection, forged in the crucible of ambition and shared dreams, transcended the boundaries of musical partnership and evolved into a passionate, albeit tumultuous, romance.

Their initial attraction was undeniable. Sonny, eleven years Cher's senior, provided stability and guidance to the young and insecure aspiring singer. Cher, with her striking beauty and undeniable talent, captivated Sonny and fueled his creative ambitions. Their relationship quickly evolved from friendship to romance, culminating in a marriage ceremony in Tijuana, Mexico, in 1964. (They later had a legal ceremony in 1969 after the birth of their Son, Chastity.)

Their personal and professional lives were deeply intertwined. They were lovers, collaborators, and business partners, their fates inextricably linked. The success of Sonny & Cher brought them fame and fortune, but it also put immense pressure on their relationship. As Cher's desire for independence grew, tensions arose, leading to clashes over creative control and personal autonomy.

Despite their love for each other, their differences became irreconcilable. Cher's yearning for individual expression clashed with Sonny's desire to maintain control. Their divorce in 1975 was a highly publicized affair, marking the end of an era both personally and professionally.

The pain of their separation was profound, but it also marked a turning point for Cher. It allowed her to fully embrace her independence and embark on a new chapter in her life and career. Despite the bitterness of their divorce, they eventually reconciled, maintaining a professional relationship and even appearing together on television. Sonny's tragic death in a skiing accident in 1998 brought a wave of grief for Cher, who delivered a moving eulogy at his funeral, acknowledging the profound impact he had on her life.

Cher's romantic life after Sonny was a tapestry of passionate encounters and fleeting connections. She was linked to a string of high-profile men, including rock stars like Gregg Allman and Gene Simmons, actors like Warren Beatty and Val Kilmer, and even a bagel baker, Rob Camilletti.

Her marriage to Gregg Allman, just days after her divorce from Sonny, was a whirlwind romance that quickly imploded. Their shared struggles with addiction and their contrasting lifestyles led to a tumultuous relationship marked by separations and reconciliations. They had a son, Elijah Blue, but ultimately divorced in 1979.

Cher's subsequent relationships were often short-lived, reflecting her independent spirit and her unwillingness to compromise her autonomy. She embraced her freedom, exploring different connections and refusing to be defined by any one relationship.

Cher's experiences with love and loss have shaped her into the resilient and independent woman she is today. She has learned valuable lessons about the complexities of relationships, the importance of self-love, and the power of forgiveness.

Her openness about her personal life, both the triumphs and the heartbreaks, has resonated with fans who admire her honesty and her refusal to conform to societal expectations. Cher's journey reminds us that love can be both exhilarating and painful, and that even in the face of loss, we can find the strength to move forward and embrace new beginnings.

A New Chapter

The 1980s marked a period of significant transformation for Cher, both personally and professionally. She shed the remnants of her disco persona and embraced a bolder, edgier image, aligning herself with the burgeoning rock scene. This reinvention proved to be a shrewd move, revitalizing her career and solidifying her status as a versatile and enduring artist.

Cher's transition to a rock-inspired sound began with her 1979 album *Take Me Home*. While it still contained elements of disco, the album incorporated a harder edge with tracks like the rock-influenced "Outrageous." This shift signaled her willingness to experiment and adapt to the changing musical landscape.

Her subsequent album, *Prisoner* (1979), further solidified this new direction. The album cover, featuring Cher in a chainmail bikini and a spiked dog collar, was a bold statement that reflected her evolving image. While the album itself received mixed reviews, it demonstrated Cher's commitment to pushing boundaries and challenging expectations.

This period also saw Cher exploring her acting talents, appearing in Broadway productions and taking on more serious film roles. This diversification allowed her to showcase her versatility and reach new audiences.

In the early 1980s, Cher collaborated with a number of prominent rock musicians, further solidifying her connection to the genre. She worked with Kiss bassist Gene Simmons, who produced her 1982 album *I Paralyze*. The album featured a harder rock sound, with tracks like the title track and "Rudy" showcasing Cher's powerful vocals and her newfound rock attitude.

She also collaborated with Black Rose, a rock band featuring members of Kiss, on the 1980 film *Foxes*. Cher's performance in the film, as a tough-talking teenager navigating the challenges of life in Los Angeles, further cemented her image as a rebellious and independent woman.

Cher's transformation extended beyond her music. She adopted a more androgynous and rebellious look, with leather jackets, ripped jeans, and elaborate tattoos replacing the flowing gowns and feathered headdresses of her disco days. Her signature black hair became even more voluminous and wild, reflecting her newfound rock 'n' roll spirit.

This image overhaul was masterminded in part by her relationship with Gene Simmons, who encouraged her to embrace a more provocative and edgy style. This transformation resonated with fans and critics alike, establishing Cher as a fashion icon who defied categorization.

Cher's reinvention in the 1980s proved to be a successful strategy. It allowed her to tap into a new fan base and revitalize her career after a period of commercial decline. Her willingness to embrace change and challenge expectations solidified her status as a versatile and enduring artist.

This period of experimentation and exploration laid the groundwork for her continued success in the decades to come. It demonstrated her ability to adapt to changing trends while remaining true to her core identity as a fearless and independent artist.

Cher's transformation in the 1980s was a bold and calculated move that paid off handsomely. By embracing a rock-inspired image and sound, she reinvented herself for a new generation of fans and solidified her status as a true icon. Her willingness to push boundaries and defy expectations cemented her legacy as one of the most versatile and enduring artists in the history of popular music.

Part 3: Conquering Hollywood

Serious Actress

While Cher had dabbled in acting throughout the 1960s and 70s, often appearing in comedic roles or projects related to her singing career, the 1980s saw her make a conscious effort to transition into more serious dramatic roles. This move, initially met with skepticism from some critics, proved to be a triumph, showcasing her versatility and establishing her as a respected actress in Hollywood.

The challenge for Cher was to overcome the public's perception of her as primarily a singer and television personality. To be taken seriously as a dramatic actress, she needed to shed the glitz and glamour associated with her pop star image and demonstrate her ability to inhabit complex, emotionally resonant characters.

She began this transition by taking on challenging roles in stage productions. In 1982, she made her Broadway debut in Robert Altman's play *Come Back to the Five and Dime, Jimmy Dean, Jimmy Dean*, playing a troubled woman with a dark past.[1] This performance garnered critical acclaim and demonstrated her ability to handle dramatic material.

Cher's breakthrough in film came with her role in the 1983 drama *Silkwood*. Directed by Mike Nichols, the film tells the true story of Karen Silkwood, a nuclear plant worker who became a whistleblower and died under mysterious circumstances.[2]

Cher's portrayal of Dolly Pelliker, Silkwood's friend and coworker, was a revelation. She delivered a nuanced and emotionally powerful performance, capturing the vulnerability and strength of a woman struggling with personal demons and fighting for justice.[3] This role earned her a Golden Globe Award for Best Supporting Actress and her first Academy Award nomination.[4]

Cher continued to challenge herself with unconventional roles, demonstrating her range and fearlessness as an actress. In the 1985 film *Mask*, she played Rusty Dennis, the fiercely protective mother of a teenage boy with craniodiaphyseal dysplasia, a rare bone disorder that causes facial deformities.

This role required Cher to shed her glamorous image and embrace a raw, unglamorous character.[5] She delivered a powerful and moving performance, conveying the love, pain, and resilience of a mother fighting for her son's acceptance. Her performance in *Mask* earned her the Best Actress award at the Cannes Film Festival and further solidified her reputation as a serious dramatic actress.[6]

Cher's transition to dramatic roles was a resounding success. She proved her ability to inhabit complex characters and deliver emotionally powerful performances, earning the respect of critics and audiences alike.[7] Her willingness to take on challenging and unconventional roles demonstrated her versatility and her commitment to her craft.

This period marked a significant turning point in Cher's career. She had successfully navigated the transition from pop star to respected actress, opening up new opportunities and solidifying her status as a multi-talented entertainer.

Cher's foray into dramatic acting was a bold and successful move. She defied expectations and proved her ability to handle complex and emotionally demanding roles. Her performances in *Silkwood* and *Mask* showcased her range and depth as an actress, earning her critical acclaim and establishing her as a force to be reckoned with in Hollywood.[8] This new chapter in her career demonstrated her versatility and her unwavering commitment to pushing boundaries and exploring new creative avenues.

Oscar Triumph

The year 1987 saw Cher starring in three high-profile films: *The Witches of Eastwick*, *Suspect*, and *Moonstruck*. It was the latter, a romantic comedy with a distinctly Italian-American flavor, that would propel her to the pinnacle of Hollywood success and cement her status as a truly versatile performer. *Moonstruck* was not just a box-office hit; it was a critical darling, earning six Academy Award nominations, including one for Cher in the Best Actress category.

In *Moonstruck*, Cher plays Loretta Castorini, a widowed Italian-American woman from Brooklyn, New York. Loretta, resigned to a life of quiet loneliness, agrees to a practical marriage with a timid man, Johnny Cammareri (played by Danny Aiello). However, her life takes an unexpected turn when she meets Ronny (Nicolas Cage), Johnny's passionate and volatile younger brother. What ensues is a whirlwind romance fueled by opera, full moons, and the simmering passions of a large, boisterous family.

The role of Loretta was perfectly suited to Cher's strengths. She brought a combination of vulnerability, strength, and dry wit to the character, creating a relatable and endearing protagonist. Loretta's journey of self-discovery resonated with audiences, particularly women who saw in her a reflection of their own desires and frustrations.

Moonstruck was met with widespread critical acclaim. Reviewers praised the film's witty dialogue, its charming performances, and its celebration of family and tradition. Cher's performance, in particular, was singled out for praise. Critics lauded her comedic timing, her emotional depth, and her ability to convey the complexities of a woman navigating love, loss, and the expectations of her culture.

The film's success translated into awards season buzz. *Moonstruck* received six Academy Award nominations, including Best Picture, Best Director, and Best Original Screenplay. Cher's nomination for Best Actress was a testament to her transformative performance and her successful transition from pop star to serious actress.

The 60th Academy Awards ceremony, held on April 11, 1988, was a night of triumph for Cher. She took home the Oscar for Best Actress, beating out formidable competition that included Glenn Close, Holly Hunter, Meryl Streep, and Sally Kirkland. Her acceptance speech was both humorous and heartfelt, acknowledging her surprise at winning and thanking those who had supported her throughout her career.

Cher's Oscar win was a watershed moment. It validated her talent as an actress and solidified her place in Hollywood history. It also served as an inspiration to women, particularly those who had been told they were "too old" or "too unconventional" to achieve success in the entertainment industry.

Moonstruck remains a beloved classic, celebrated for its humor, its heart, and its memorable characters. Cher's performance continues to be regarded as one of her finest, a testament to her ability to inhabit a role fully and bring it to life with authenticity and charm.

The film's success had a profound impact on Cher's career. It opened doors to new opportunities and allowed her to command leading roles in a variety of genres. It also cemented her status as a cultural icon, a woman who defied expectations and achieved success on her own terms.

Cher's Oscar win for *Moonstruck* was a culmination of years of hard work, dedication, and a willingness to take risks. It was a recognition of her talent, her versatility, and her ability to connect with audiences on a deeply emotional level. This triumph solidified her place in Hollywood history and served as an inspiration to aspiring actors and actresses everywhere. *Moonstruck* remains a testament to the power of storytelling, the magic of cinema, and the enduring appeal of a truly gifted performer.

Box Office Draw

While her Oscar win for *Moonstruck* solidified Cher's status as a serious actress, she didn't abandon lighter fare. The late 1980s and early 1990s saw her continue to demonstrate her box office appeal in a variety of films, proving her ability to attract audiences and deliver memorable performances across different genres.

In *Mermaids*, Cher starred alongside Winona Ryder and a young Christina Ricci in this quirky coming-of-age story. Cher plays Rachel Flax, a free-spirited single mother who relocates her two daughters to a small Massachusetts town in the 1960s. Rachel, with her flamboyant style and unconventional approach to life, clashes with her more conservative surroundings and her teenage daughter Charlotte (Ryder), who longs for stability and normalcy.

Mermaids was a critical and commercial success, praised for its heartwarming story, its strong performances, and its nostalgic portrayal of the 1960s. Cher's performance as the eccentric and loving Rachel was a highlight, showcasing her comedic timing and her ability to portray a complex and flawed character with depth and empathy. The film solidified her appeal as a bankable star who could carry a film with her charisma and talent.

Released the same year as *Moonstruck*, *The Witches of Eastwick* saw Cher join forces with Michelle Pfeiffer and Susan Sarandon in this supernatural comedy. The film, based on the novel by John Updike, tells the story of three women in a small New England town who unknowingly possess magical powers. Their lives are turned upside down when a mysterious and charismatic stranger, Daryl Van Horne (Jack Nicholson), arrives in town, awakening their latent abilities and unleashing a whirlwind of supernatural events.

Cher plays Alexandra Medford, a sculptor and single mother. Her performance as the witty and independent Alexandra was a perfect complement to Pfeiffer's and Sarandon's characters, creating a dynamic trio of strong female leads. The film was a box office hit, thanks in part to its star-studded cast and its blend of comedy, fantasy, and romance. Cher's presence in the film further solidified her appeal as a draw for audiences, demonstrating her ability to hold her own alongside other A-list actors.

While *Mermaids* and *The Witches of Eastwick* stand out as notable successes, Cher continued to appear in a variety of films throughout the 1990s and beyond. She took on roles in dramas like *Tea with Mussolini* (1999), comedies like *Stuck on You* (2003), and even lent her voice to animated films like *Zookeeper* (2011).

Her film choices reflected her eclectic tastes and her willingness to experiment with different genres and characters. While not all of her films were critical or commercial hits, Cher consistently brought her unique charisma and talent to each role, ensuring that her presence on screen was always memorable.

Cher's continued success in films like *Mermaids* and *The Witches of Eastwick* demonstrated her staying power as a box office draw. She proved her ability to attract audiences across different genres and demographics, solidifying her status as a versatile and bankable star. Her film career, spanning several decades, is a testament to her talent, her charisma, and her enduring appeal as an entertainer.

Cher's ability to transition seamlessly between dramatic roles and lighter fare showcased her range and her appeal to a wide audience. Films like *Mermaids* and *The Witches of Eastwick* not only entertained but also provided strong female characters that resonated with viewers. Her continued success in Hollywood cemented her position as a true icon, capable of captivating audiences with her talent and personality, regardless of the genre.

Broadway Bound

While Cher was already a household name thanks to her music and film career, she continued to seek new challenges and creative outlets. In the early 1980s, she set her sights on Broadway, making her stage debut in a production that would further demonstrate her versatility and solidify her reputation as a multi-talented performer.

Cher's Broadway debut came in 1982 with the play *Come Back to the Five and Dime, Jimmy Dean, Jimmy Dean*. Written by Ed Graczyk, the play is a character-driven drama set in a small Texas town. It tells the story of a group of women who reunite 20 years after their idol, James Dean, filmed a movie in their town. As they reminisce about the past, old wounds are reopened, and secrets are revealed.

Cher took on the role of Sissy, a waitress at the local five and dime store. Sissy is a complex character, harboring a secret that has haunted her for years. The role required Cher to tap into her dramatic abilities, and she delivered a powerful and nuanced performance that garnered critical acclaim.

The play, directed by Robert Altman, also featured a talented ensemble cast, including Sandy Dennis, Karen Black, and Kathy Bates. It was a critical success, praised for its strong performances and its exploration of themes like memory, identity, and the passage of time.

The success of the play led to a film adaptation, also directed by Robert Altman, later that same year. Cher reprised her role as Sissy in the film, which retained much of the play's dialogue and emotional intensity. The film version of *Come Back to the Five and Dime, Jimmy Dean, Jimmy Dean* allowed Cher to showcase her dramatic talents to a wider audience and further solidified her reputation as a versatile actress.

Cher's foray into Broadway was a significant step in her career. It allowed her to explore a new creative avenue and challenge herself as a performer. Her performance in *Come Back to the Five and Dime, Jimmy Dean, Jimmy Dean*demonstrated her ability to handle complex dramatic material and earned her the respect of the theater community.

This experience also helped her to further develop her acting skills, which she would continue to utilize in her subsequent film roles. The discipline and focus required for stage acting undoubtedly contributed to her growth as an actress and her ability to inhabit a wide range of characters.

While Cher's Broadway debut remains her most notable stage performance, she has occasionally returned to the theater throughout her career. In 2002, she embarked on a farewell tour that included a limited engagement on Broadway, showcasing her musical talents and her enduring appeal as a live performer.

Cher's venture into the world of Broadway with *Come Back to the Five and Dime, Jimmy Dean, Jimmy Dean* was a successful and significant chapter in her career. It demonstrated her versatility as a performer and her willingness to embrace new challenges. Her stage debut allowed her to showcase her dramatic talents and further solidified her reputation as a multi-talented entertainer capable of captivating audiences in any medium.

Part 4: The Icon Emerges

"Believe" and the Dance Music Era

The late 1990s witnessed a remarkable resurgence in Cher's music career, propelled by the global smash hit "Believe." This infectious dance-pop anthem not only topped charts worldwide but also introduced Cher to a new generation of fans, solidifying her status as a timeless icon.

In 1998, at the age of 52, Cher released her 22nd studio album, *Believe*. The album marked a departure from her previous work, embracing the sounds of electronic dance music that were dominating the pop landscape. This strategic shift in musical direction proved to be a masterstroke, aligning her with contemporary trends while showcasing her ability to adapt and evolve.

The album's title track, "Believe," became an instant sensation. Its pulsating beat, catchy melody, and empowering lyrics resonated with audiences worldwide. The song's distinctive vocal effect, achieved through the use of Auto-Tune, became a defining characteristic of the track and a widely imitated trend in pop music.

"Believe" quickly climbed the charts, reaching the number one spot in over 23 countries. It became the best-selling single of 1999 in the United States and the United Kingdom, breaking numerous records in the process. The song's success propelled the *Believe* album to multi-platinum status, further solidifying Cher's commercial appeal.

The song's popularity transcended age barriers, introducing Cher to a younger generation who may have been unfamiliar with her earlier work. "Believe" became an anthem of empowerment and self-affirmation, its message of overcoming heartbreak resonating with listeners of all ages.

The use of Auto-Tune on "Believe" was groundbreaking at the time. The effect, which digitally corrected Cher's vocals, created a robotic, otherworldly sound that was both distinctive and captivating. While initially intended to subtly correct pitch imperfections, the producers embraced the effect's unique quality, making it a prominent feature of the song.

This innovative use of technology became a hallmark of late 1990s and early 2000s pop music, influencing countless artists and producers. "Believe" paved the way for the widespread use of Auto-Tune in popular music, demonstrating its potential to create unique and memorable vocal effects.

The success of "Believe" solidified Cher's status as a true icon, capable of reinventing herself and achieving success across different eras and musical genres. The song's enduring popularity is a testament to its catchy melody, its empowering message, and its innovative use of technology.

Cher's ability to connect with audiences of all ages, her willingness to embrace new sounds, and her refusal to be defined by age or expectations have contributed to her longevity in the ever-changing world of pop music.

"Believe" marked a pivotal moment in Cher's career, showcasing her ability to adapt to contemporary trends while retaining her unique artistic identity. The song's global success, its innovative use of technology, and its enduring appeal solidified Cher's status as a true icon, capable of transcending generations and musical genres. "Believe" remains a testament to Cher's resilience, her artistry, and her ability to continually surprise and delight audiences worldwide.

Fashion Forward

Cher's impact on fashion is undeniable. She has consistently pushed boundaries, defied conventions, and set trends throughout her decades-long career.[1] Her fearless approach to style, her willingness to experiment, and her innate sense of self-expression have made her a true fashion icon, inspiring designers, stylists, and fans worldwide.

Cher's early fashion choices reflected the bohemian spirit of the 1960s. She embraced flowing silhouettes, bold prints, and ethnic-inspired accessories. Her long, flowing hair, often adorned with flowers or headbands, became a signature look. She favored bell bottoms, peasant blouses, and vests, creating a style that was both feminine and free-spirited.

Her partnership with Sonny Bono further amplified her fashion influence. Their contrasting styles – Sonny's clean-cut look juxtaposed with Cher's more unconventional attire – created a visual dynamic that captivated audiences. They became fashion icons for a generation embracing change and challenging traditional norms.

Cher's collaboration with designer Bob Mackie in the 1970s and 80s produced some of her most iconic looks. Mackie's flamboyant designs, often featuring intricate beading, feathers, and sequins, perfectly complemented Cher's bold personality and stage presence. Her appearances on *The Sonny & Cher Comedy Hour* and her concert performances became fashion spectacles, showcasing Mackie's creativity and Cher's willingness to embrace the avant-garde.

From the sheer beaded gown she wore to the 1974 Met Gala to the Native

61

American-inspired headdress she donned for her 1986 "I Found Someone" music video, Cher's collaborations with Mackie pushed the boundaries of fashion and cemented her status as a style innovator.

In the 1980s, Cher's style evolved to reflect her rock-inspired music and her more rebellious persona. She embraced leather jackets, ripped jeans, and fishnet stockings, creating a look that was both edgy and glamorous.[7] Her signature black hair became even more voluminous and wild, and she often sported elaborate tattoos.

This transformation, influenced in part by her relationship with Gene Simmons, showcased her ability to adapt to changing trends while remaining true to her individual style. She continued to collaborate with Bob Mackie, but her looks became more streamlined and androgynous, reflecting her evolving image.

Cher's influence on fashion extends far beyond any specific era or trend. Her fearless approach to style, her willingness to experiment, and her ability to make a statement have inspired generations of designers, stylists, and fashion enthusiasts.

Her red carpet appearances continue to generate headlines, whether she's sporting a sheer beaded gown or a daringly revealing ensemble. Her fashion choices are often bold and unexpected, but they always reflect her confidence and her unique sense of self-expression.

Cher's impact on fashion can be seen in the work of countless designers and stylists who have been inspired by her fearless approach to style. Her influence is evident in the resurgence of bohemian trends, the embrace of bold prints and embellishments, and the celebration of individuality and self-expression through fashion.

Cher's enduring status as a style icon is a testament to her ability to transcend trends and remain relevant across decades. She has consistently pushed boundaries, challenged conventions, and inspired millions to embrace their own unique style.

Cher's fashion legacy is one of fearless experimentation, bold self-expression, and enduring influence.[8] She has consistently set trends, defied expectations, and inspired generations with her unique approach to style.[9] From her bohemian beginnings to her rock 'n' roll edge and her continued red carpet dominance, Cher remains a true fashion icon, a testament to the power of personal style and the enduring appeal of a woman who dares to be different.

Activism and Advocacy

Cher's influence extends far beyond the realms of music and entertainment.[1] Throughout her career, she has used her platform to speak out on social and political issues, championing causes close to her heart and lending her voice to those often marginalized.[2] Her activism, particularly in the areas of LGBTQ+ rights and HIV/AIDS awareness, has made her a powerful advocate for change and a beacon of hope for many.

Cher's rebellious spirit and her willingness to challenge societal norms were evident from the early days of her career. Her unconventional fashion choices and her outspoken personality defied expectations and paved the way for greater acceptance of individuality and self-expression.

In the 1960s and 70s, she challenged traditional gender roles with her androgynous style and her assertive persona. She spoke out against the Vietnam War and supported the civil rights movement, aligning herself with progressive causes and using her platform to raise awareness.

Cher's advocacy for LGBTQ+ rights is deeply personal. Her own daughter, Chastity (now Chaz Bono), came out as a lesbian in 1995 and later transitioned to male. Cher's unwavering support for her child's journey made her a powerful ally for the LGBTQ+ community.

She has spoken out against discrimination and prejudice, advocating for equal rights and acceptance for all individuals, regardless of their sexual orientation or gender identity.[3] She has participated in numerous rallies and marches, lent her voice to public service announcements, and used her social media presence to raise awareness and promote understanding.

Her advocacy has earned her recognition from various LGBTQ+ organizations. In 2005, she received the GLAAD Vanguard Award for her contributions to promoting equality and acceptance. Her unwavering support for the LGBTQ+ community has made her a role model for parents and allies, demonstrating the importance of love and acceptance in the face of prejudice.[4]

The HIV/AIDS epidemic hit close to home for Cher, who lost many friends and colleagues to the disease. In the 1980s and 90s, when stigma and misinformation surrounding HIV/AIDS were rampant, she used her platform to raise awareness and combat prejudice.

She publicly supported organizations like amfAR (The Foundation for AIDS Research) and participated in fundraising events and public awareness campaigns.[5] She spoke out against discrimination against people living with HIV/AIDS and advocated for increased funding for research and treatment.[6]

Her activism helped to destigmatize the disease and promote compassion and understanding. Her willingness to speak out during a time when many were afraid to even mention HIV/AIDS made her a crucial voice in the fight against the epidemic.

Cher's commitment to social and political activism continues to this day. She uses her social media presence to speak out on issues like climate change, gun control, and social justice. She remains a vocal advocate for marginalized communities and a powerful voice for change.[7]

Her activism is an integral part of her legacy, demonstrating her commitment to using her platform for good and inspiring others to do the same. Cher's willingness to speak truth to power, her compassion for those in need, and her unwavering support for equality and justice have made her a true icon, not just in the world of entertainment, but in the fight for a better world.

Cher's activism and advocacy are evidence to her courage, her compassion, and her commitment to making a difference. Her outspokenness on social and political issues, particularly in the areas of LGBTQ+ rights and HIV/AIDS awareness, has made her a powerful force for change and an inspiration to millions.[8] Her willingness to use her platform to speak out against injustice and advocate for those often marginalized has cemented her legacy as not just a talented entertainer, but a true humanitarian.

The Farewell Tours (That Never End)

Cher's relationship with touring is a evidence to her enduring appeal as a live performer and her deep connection with her fans. She's renowned for her spectacular stage shows, her elaborate costumes, and her ability to command an audience with her powerful vocals and magnetic personality. While she's embarked on several "farewell" tours throughout her career, her love for the stage and her fans' insatiable appetite for her performances have kept her coming back for more.

Cher's concert tours have always been more than just musical performances; they're theatrical productions that combine music, dance, costume changes, and storytelling. From her early tours with Sonny Bono to her elaborate solo productions, she's consistently raised the bar for live entertainment.

Her tours in the 1970s and 80s were known for their extravagant costumes, often designed by Bob Mackie, and their theatrical elements. She incorporated elaborate sets, pyrotechnics, and even aerial stunts into her shows, creating a visual spectacle that captivated audiences.

In 2002, Cher embarked on what was billed as her "farewell" tour, the "Living Proof: The Farewell Tour." The tour, which spanned three years and included over 300 shows, was a massive success, breaking records and earning critical acclaim.

However, despite its name, the "Farewell Tour" was not the end of Cher's touring career. Due to popular demand, she extended the tour multiple times and even embarked on subsequent tours in 2008 and 2014.

Cher's enduring connection with her fans is a key factor in her continued success as a live performer. She has a loyal following that spans generations, drawn to her music, her personality, and her ability to create a shared experience during her concerts.

Her shows are known for their intimate moments, where she interacts with the audience, shares personal anecdotes, and expresses her gratitude for their support. She creates a sense of connection that goes beyond the music, making her fans feel like they're part of something special.

In 2018, Cher embarked on yet another tour, dubbed the "Here We Go Again Tour." The tour, which featured songs from her album *Dancing Queen* (a collection of ABBA covers), as well as classic hits from throughout her career, was another massive success, proving that her appeal as a live performer remains as strong as ever.

The "Here We Go Again Tour" showcased Cher's ability to adapt and evolve, incorporating contemporary elements into her shows while still delivering the spectacle and intimacy that her fans have come to expect.

Cher's concert tours are a evidence to her enduring talent, her showmanship, and her connection with her fans. She has consistently delivered unforgettable live experiences, combining music, spectacle, and personal connection to create a lasting impact on audiences worldwide.

Her "farewell" tours that never quite end are a testament to her love for the stage and her dedication to her fans. As long as there's an audience eager to see her perform, it's likely that Cher will continue to grace the stage with her presence, defying age and expectations and cementing her legacy as one of the greatest live performers of all time.

Cher's legendary concert tours are evidence to her enduring appeal as a live performer and her deep connection with her fans. She has consistently delivered spectacular shows that combine music, dance, costume changes, and storytelling, creating unforgettable experiences for audiences worldwide. Her "farewell" tours that never quite end are a testament to her love for the stage and her dedication to her fans, ensuring that her legacy as a live performer will continue for years to come.

Part 5: The Legacy of Cher

A Timeless Star

Cher's influence transcends the boundaries of any single medium.[1] She's a true multi-hyphenate, a singer, actress, and entertainer who has left an indelible mark on music, film, and popular culture.[2] Her impact is not just defined by her artistic achievements, but also by her fearless personality, her groundbreaking fashion choices, and her willingness to challenge societal norms.[3]

Cher's musical career spans over six decades, and she has consistently pushed the boundaries of pop music, experimenting with different genres and styles.[4] From her early success with Sonny Bono to her solo hits like "Believe" and "If I Could Turn Back Time," she has delivered a string of iconic songs that have become part of the cultural lexicon.[5]

Her influence on music extends beyond her own recordings.[6] She has inspired countless artists with her vocal prowess, her stage presence, and her willingness to take risks.[7] Her impact can be seen in the work of contemporary pop stars who embrace her fearless attitude and her commitment to self-expression.[8]

Cher's transition from pop star to respected actress is a testament to her talent and versatility. She has delivered memorable performances in a wide range of films, from dramas like *Silkwood* and *Mask* to comedies like *Moonstruck* and *Mermaids*.

Her Oscar win for *Moonstruck* solidified her status as a serious actress and opened doors to new opportunities. She has continued to challenge herself with diverse roles, demonstrating her ability to inhabit complex characters and connect with audiences on an emotional level.

Cher's impact on popular culture is undeniable. Her fearless personality, her groundbreaking fashion choices, and her outspoken views have made her a symbol of individuality and self-expression.[9]

She has consistently challenged societal norms and defied expectations, paving the way for greater acceptance of diversity and individuality.[10] Her influence can be seen in the way people embrace their own unique style, express their opinions without fear, and challenge the status quo.[11]

One of the defining characteristics of Cher's career is her ability to reinvent herself.[12] She has constantly evolved, adapting to changing trends and embracing new challenges.[13] This willingness to change and grow has kept her relevant across decades and has inspired others to embrace change and pursue their own passions.[14]

Cher has been a role model for women throughout her career. She has achieved success in a male-dominated industry, defied ageism, and demonstrated that women can be strong, independent, and successful on their own terms.[15]

Her fearlessness, her resilience, and her commitment to her own vision have inspired countless women to pursue their dreams and challenge limitations.[16]

Cher's influence extends far beyond the borders of the United States.[17] She is a global icon, recognized and admired worldwide for her music, her films, and her impact on popular culture.[18]

Her music has topped charts around the world, her films have been seen by millions, and her fashion choices have influenced trends globally.[19] She is a true international star, whose impact will be felt for generations to come.[20]

Cher's impact on music, film, and popular culture is profound and far-reaching.[21] She is a true multi-hyphenate, a pioneer of pop music, a versatile actress, and a fashion icon who has inspired millions with her fearless personality, her groundbreaking style, and her willingness to challenge societal norms.[22] Her legacy is one of reinvention, resilience, and a commitment to individuality, ensuring that she will remain a timeless star for years to come.[23]

Breaking Barriers

Cher's legacy extends beyond her artistic achievements. She stands as a powerful symbol of female empowerment in an industry often dominated by men. Throughout her career, she has defied expectations, shattered stereotypes, and paved the way for generations of women in entertainment. Her influence is particularly notable in her defiance of ageism, proving that women can remain relevant, creative, and successful throughout their lives.[1]

From the outset, Cher challenged the prevailing norms of the entertainment industry. In the 1960s, as one half of Sonny & Cher, she defied traditional gender roles with her assertive personality and her unconventional fashion choices. She refused to be relegated to the background, demanding equal footing with her male counterpart and contributing significantly to their creative partnership.

As a solo artist, she continued to push boundaries. She asserted control over her music and image, refusing to be pigeonholed or constrained by industry expectations. She embraced a variety of musical styles, from folk-rock to disco to dance-pop, demonstrating her versatility and refusing to be defined by any single genre.

Perhaps Cher's most significant contribution to breaking barriers is her defiance of ageism. In an industry that often favors youth and novelty, she has consistently proven that women can remain relevant, creative, and successful throughout their lives.[2]

She has continued to release music, tour the world, and act in films well into her seventies. Her ability to adapt to changing trends, embrace new technologies, and connect with audiences of all ages is a testament to her enduring talent and her refusal to be limited by societal expectations about aging.

Cher's impact on women in the entertainment industry is profound. She has served as a role model for generations of female artists, demonstrating that women can be strong, independent, and successful on their own terms.

Her fearlessness, her resilience, and her commitment to her own vision have inspired countless women to pursue their dreams and challenge limitations.[3] She has shown that age is not a barrier to creativity or success, and that women can continue to evolve and reinvent themselves throughout their lives.

Cher's legacy is one of empowerment, challenging stereotypes, and breaking down barriers.[4] She has paved the way for greater representation and acceptance of women in the entertainment industry, demonstrating that women can achieve success on their own terms, regardless of age or expectations.

Her influence can be seen in the growing number of female artists who are taking control of their careers, expressing their individuality, and defying ageism. Cher has shown that women can be powerful forces in the entertainment industry, and her legacy will continue to inspire generations of women to pursue their dreams and challenge the status quo.

Cher's impact on women in the entertainment industry is undeniable. She has challenged the status quo, defied ageism, and inspired generations of female artists to pursue their dreams and break down barriers.[5] Her legacy is one of empowerment, demonstrating that women can be successful, creative, and relevant throughout their lives.[6] She is a true trailblazer, and her influence will continue to be felt for years to come.

The "Goddess of Pop

The moniker "Goddess of Pop" is more than just a catchy title for Cher; it's a reflection of her enduring appeal, her influence on music, and her unique position in pop culture. She's earned this title through decades of groundbreaking work, consistently defying expectations and reinventing herself while remaining a relevant and captivating force in the music industry.

Cher's place in music history is marked by a series of firsts and a fearless defiance of convention. She was one of the first female artists to achieve mainstream success in a rock and roll landscape dominated by men. With Sonny Bono, she pioneered a new sound that blended folk, pop, and rock, capturing the spirit of the 1960s youth movement.

As a solo artist, she continued to break barriers. She was one of the first female artists to embrace the disco sound in the 1970s, achieving massive success with hits like "Gypsys, Tramps & Thieves" and "Half-Breed." She later reinvented herself as a rock-inspired performer in the 1980s, collaborating with artists like Gene Simmons and adopting a more androgynous style.

In the late 1990s, she once again defied expectations with the dance-pop anthem "Believe," which showcased her ability to adapt to contemporary trends while retaining her unique artistic identity. The song's innovative use of Auto-Tune paved the way for a new wave of electronic pop music.

Cher's enduring appeal lies in her ability to connect with audiences on a personal level. Her music often explores themes of love, loss, and empowerment, resonating with listeners across generations. She's not afraid to be vulnerable, sharing her own experiences and struggles through her songs.

Her willingness to evolve and experiment has also contributed to her longevity. She has never been afraid to take risks, embracing new sounds and styles while remaining true to her core identity. This constant evolution has kept her music fresh and relevant, attracting new fans while retaining her loyal following.

Cher's impact extends beyond her music. She is a cultural icon, known for her fashion choices, her outspoken personality, and her activism. She has consistently challenged societal norms and defied expectations, becoming a symbol of individuality and self-expression.

Her influence can be seen in the work of countless artists who have been inspired by her music, her style, and her fearless attitude. She has paved the way for greater acceptance of diversity and individuality in the entertainment industry and beyond.

Cher's place in music history is secure. She is a true pioneer, a trailblazer who has broken barriers and defied conventions throughout her career. Her music has touched millions of lives, and her influence on pop culture is undeniable.

She has earned the title "Goddess of Pop" through her talent, her hard work, and her unwavering commitment to her artistic vision. Her legacy will continue to inspire generations of musicians and entertainers, ensuring that her place in music history is forever cemented.

Cher's enduring appeal, her groundbreaking achievements, and her constant evolution have earned her the title "Goddess of Pop." She is a true icon, a pioneer who has defied expectations and broken barriers throughout her career. Her influence on music, fashion, and popular culture is undeniable, ensuring that her place in music history is forever secure.

Part 6: Discography, Filmography and Achievements

Discography

Cher's discography is evidence to her longevity, versatility, and enduring appeal as a musical artist. Spanning over six decades, her musical output encompasses a wide range of genres and styles, reflecting her willingness to experiment, evolve, and connect with audiences across generations. From her early folk-rock influences to her forays into disco, dance-pop, and even ABBA covers, Cher's discography is a rich and varied tapestry of musical exploration.

Cher's early recordings were heavily influenced by the folk-rock movement of the 1960s. Her debut solo album, *All I*

Really Want to Do (1965), featured covers of popular folk songs, showcasing her interpretive skills and her ability to connect with the youth culture of the time.

Her partnership with Sonny Bono led to a string of successful albums that blended folk, pop, and rock elements. Their signature sound, characterized by Sonny's songwriting and Cher's distinctive vocals, produced iconic hits like "I Got You Babe" and "The Beat Goes On." These songs captured the spirit of the 1960s and solidified their status as pop culture icons.

As a solo artist, Cher continued to explore a variety of musical styles. In the 1970s, she embraced the disco sound, achieving massive success with albums like *Gypsys, Tramps & Thieves* (1971) and *Half-Breed* (1973). These albums showcased her vocal prowess and her ability to connect with a wider audience.

She continued to experiment throughout the 1970s and 80s, incorporating elements of rock, pop, and even country into her music. Albums like *Take Me Home* (1979) and *Prisoner* (1979) reflected her evolving tastes and her growing confidence as an artist.

The late 1990s saw a resurgence in Cher's music career with the release of the dance-pop anthem "Believe." This global smash hit introduced her to a new generation of fans and solidified her status as a timeless icon.

Her subsequent albums, such as *Living Proof* (2001) and *Closer to the Truth* (2013), continued to showcase her versatility and her ability to adapt to contemporary trends while retaining her unique artistic identity.

In 2018, she surprised fans with *Dancing Queen*, an album of ABBA covers that demonstrated her love for the Swedish pop group and her ability to put her own spin on classic songs.

Cher's discography is extensive and diverse, encompassing 26 studio albums, numerous compilation albums, and countless singles. Her music has topped charts around the world, earning her numerous awards and accolades.

Her most successful albums include:

- *Gypsys, Tramps & Thieves* (1971)
- *Half-Breed* (1973)
- *Dark Lady* (1974)
- I Paralyze (1982)
- *Believe* (1998)
- *Living Proof* (2001)

Her most popular singles include:

- "I Got You Babe" (with Sonny & Cher) (1965)
- "Gypsys, Tramps & Thieves" (1971)
- "Half-Breed" (1973)
- "If I Could Turn Back Time" (1989)
- "Believe" (1998) e.t.c

Cher's discography is evidence to her enduring appeal as a musical artist. Her willingness to experiment, evolve, and connect with audiences across generations has ensured her longevity in the ever-changing world of pop music.

Her music has served as a soundtrack to countless lives, providing comfort, inspiration, and joy to millions of fans worldwide. Her discography is a rich and varied tapestry of musical exploration, a testament to her talent, her creativity, and her unwavering commitment to her artistic vision.

Cher's discography is a reflection of her remarkable career, showcasing her versatility, her longevity, and her enduring appeal as a musical artist. From her early folk-rock influences to her forays into disco, dance-pop, and beyond, her music has touched millions of lives and solidified her place in music history. Her extensive and diverse catalog is evidence to her talent, her creativity, and her unwavering commitment to her artistic vision.

Filmography

Cher's filmography is a testament to her versatility and her enduring presence in Hollywood.[1] Spanning over five decades, her film career has seen her take on a wide range of roles, from comedic cameos to dramatic leading roles that earned her critical acclaim and prestigious awards.[2] Her filmography showcases her ability to inhabit diverse characters, connect with audiences, and leave a lasting impact on the world of cinema.[3]

Cher's early film appearances were often tied to her musical career. She and Sonny Bono starred in *Good Times* (1967), a musical comedy that capitalized on their popularity as a singing duo.[4] While the film was not a critical success, it showcased their on-screen chemistry and their appeal as entertainers.

She also appeared in *Chastity* (1969), a drama that attempted to showcase her acting abilities beyond the musical genre.[5]However, the film was poorly received, and it wasn't until the 1980s that Cher truly began to establish herself as a serious actress.

The 1980s marked a turning point in Cher's film career. She took on challenging roles in films like *Silkwood* (1983) and *Mask* (1985), demonstrating her ability to handle dramatic material and portray complex characters with depth and nuance.[6] These performances earned her critical acclaim and award nominations, solidifying her reputation as a versatile actress.[7]

Cher's performance in *Moonstruck* (1987) catapulted her to the pinnacle of Hollywood success. Her portrayal of Loretta Castorini, a widowed Italian-American woman who finds love unexpectedly, earned her an Academy Award for Best Actress.[8] This win cemented her status as a leading lady and opened doors to a wider range of roles.

Following her Oscar win, Cher continued to appear in a variety of films, demonstrating her ability to attract audiences and deliver memorable performances across different genres.[9] She starred in the coming-of-age comedy-drama *Mermaids*(1990) alongside Winona Ryder and Christina Ricci, showcasing her comedic timing and her ability to portray a complex and flawed character with empathy.[10]

She also joined forces with Michelle Pfeiffer and Susan Sarandon in the supernatural comedy *The Witches of Eastwick*(1987), holding her own alongside other A-list actors and contributing to the film's box office success.[11]

Cher's film career has continued to evolve, with appearances in dramas like

Tea with Mussolini (1999), comedies like *Stuck on You* (2003), and even voice acting in animated films like *Zookeeper* (2011). While not all of her films have been critical or commercial hits, Cher consistently brings her unique charisma and talent to each role, ensuring that her presence on screen is always memorable.

Here are some of the key films in Cher's filmography:

- *Good Times* (1967)
- *Chastity* (1969)
- *Silkwood* (1983)
- *Mask* (1985)
- *The Witches of Eastwick* (1987)
- *Moonstruck* (1987)
- *Mermaids* (1990)
- *Tea with Mussolini* (1999)
- *Stuck on You* (2003)
- *Zookeeper* (2011)

Cher's filmography is evidence to her versatility, her talent, and her enduring appeal as an actress. She has successfully navigated the transition from pop star to respected actress, delivering memorable performances in a wide range of films. Her ability to connect with audiences, her willingness to take on diverse roles, and her undeniable charisma have ensured her lasting presence in Hollywood and her continued contribution to the world of cinema.

Cher's filmography is a rich and varied tapestry of cinematic achievements, showcasing her talent, her versatility, and her enduring appeal as an actress.[23] From her early appearances in musical films to her Oscar-winning performance in *Moonstruck* and her continued presence in Hollywood, her film career is a testament to her ability to captivate audiences and leave a lasting impact on the world of cinema.

Achievements

Cher's career has been marked by a remarkable collection of awards and nominations, spanning music, television, and film.[1] This impressive array of accolades reflects her versatility, her impact on popular culture, and her enduring appeal as an entertainer.[2] From the Grammys to the Oscars, Cher has consistently been recognized for her talent, her creativity, and her contribution to the world of entertainment.[3]

Cher's musical achievements have been recognized by some of the most prestigious awards in the industry.[4] She has won a Grammy Award, three Golden Globe Awards, and a Billboard Music Award, among others.[5] Her Grammy win came in 2000 for Best Dance Recording for her iconic hit "Believe."[6] This song also earned her a World Music Award for World's Best-Selling Single.

She has received numerous Billboard Music Awards, including the prestigious

Icon Award in 2017, recognizing her enduring influence on the music industry.[7] Her other Billboard Music Awards include Top Female Artist (1999) and Top Dance/Electronic Artist (2002).

Cher's television career has also been decorated with awards.[8] She has won an Emmy Award and three Golden Globe Awards for her work on television.[9] Her Emmy win came in 1974 for Outstanding Variety Series for *The Sonny & Cher Comedy Hour*. This show also earned her a Golden Globe Award for Best Performance by an Actress in a Television Series - Musical or Comedy in the same year.[10]

Cher's transition to film acting brought her even more critical acclaim and awards recognition.[11] She has won an Academy Award, a Cannes Film Festival Award, and three Golden Globe Awards for her film work.[12] Her Oscar win came in 1988 for Best Actress for her role in *Moonstruck*.[13] This performance also earned her a Golden Globe Award for Best Actress - Motion Picture Musical or Comedy.

She received a Golden Globe Award for Best Supporting Actress - Motion Picture for her role in *Silkwood* (1983) and was nominated for an Oscar for Best Supporting Actress for the same role.[14] Her performance in *Mask* (1985) earned her the Best Actress Award at the Cannes Film Festival.[15]

In addition to her competitive awards, Cher has received numerous honorary awards and recognitions.[16] She was inducted into the Rock and Roll Hall of Fame in 2001 as part of Sonny & Cher. She has also received Kennedy Center Honors (2018) and a star on the Hollywood Walk of Fame.[17]

The Council of Fashion Designers of America (CFDA) honored her with a Fashion Icon Award in 2010, recognizing her influence on the fashion industry.[18]

Cher's extensive collection of awards and nominations is a testament to her talent, her versatility, and her enduring impact on the entertainment industry.[19] She has been recognized for her achievements in music, television, and film, solidifying her status as a true icon.[20]

Her awards reflect not only her artistic accomplishments but also her willingness to challenge conventions, break barriers, and inspire generations of artists and entertainers. Her legacy of recognition is a testament to her enduring appeal and her lasting contribution to the world of entertainment.

Cher's awards and nominations represent a remarkable legacy of recognition, spanning her achievements in music, television, and film.[21] From Grammy Awards to an Academy Award, she has consistently been honored for her talent, her creativity, and her contribution to the world of entertainment.[22] Her impressive collection of accolades reflects her versatility, her impact on popular culture, and her enduring appeal as an entertainer.